2—4—6—8
HOW THOSE
KIDS COMMUNICATE!

Dear Dad,
Our new counselor, Leon, really loves nature.
All he ever talks about is going outside to get some grass.

Your son,
Roger

Dear Mom and Dad,
I like camp very much but frankly I don't want to get emotionally involved.

Love,
Anne

AND MORE, MORE!

More Humor from SIGNET

Hip Kids' Letters From Camp

Collected by
BILL ADLER

Illustrated by
Howie Schneider

A SIGNET BOOK from
NEW AMERICAN LIBRARY
TIMES MIRROR

Library of Congress Catalog Card Number: 75-142399

Published by arrangement with William Morrow and
Company, Inc.

First Printing
Second Printing
Third Printing
Fourth Printing
Fifth Printing
Sixth Printing
Seventh Printing
Eighth Printing
Ninth Printing
Tenth Printing

 SIGNET TRADEMARK REG. U.S. PAT. OFF. AND FOREIGN COUNTRIES
REGISTERED TRADEMARK—MARCA REGISTRADA
HECHO EN CHICAGO, U.S.A.

SIGNET, SIGNET CLASSICS, SIGNETTE, MENTOR
and PLUME BOOKS are published by The New American
Library, Inc.,
1301 Avenue of the Americas, New York, New York 10019

First Printing, May, 1973

PRINTED IN THE UNITED STATES OF AMERICA

Introduction

The original *Letters from Camp* was published in 1960. That was over ten years ago and yet it seems like a hundred when you consider what kids were like then and what they are like today.

For better or worse, our summer campers are like no summer campers before them. They're more hip, more worldly, with stronger opinions and maturer attitudes. The generation gap has reached into the restful pines of the New Hampshire hills and into the placid lakes of the Pocono Mountains.

Not only have summer camps changed. So have the occupants. With the help of our many friends, we have been able to compile this book, *Letters from Camp*—1970's version. If you happen to be one of the hundreds of thousands of people who purchased the original *Letters from Camp* in 1960, please don't get out your copy to compare these letters from camp with that first edition. The change may shock you.

Bill Adler
New York City

Hip Kids'
Letters
From Camp

Dear Folks,
   They don't have any dances
here anymore.
   Last night we had our
first love-in.

                Your daughter,
                Barbara

Dear Dad,
   Every night before we go to sleep, our counselor reads us a story to help us sleep better.
   Last night he read to us from the "Quotations of Chairman Mao".
            Your son,
            Peter

Dear Mom and Dad,
   We played cowboys and Indians at camp. We flipped a coin and the losers had to be the cowboys.
            Love,
            Raymond

Dear Mom and Dad,
    I've learned a lot at camp.
Yesterday one of the seniors
taught me how to avoid
getting busted.
                    Love,
                    Junior

Dear Mother,
    I don't want to be a summer
camper anymore.
    I just want to be a flower
child.
            Your loving daughter,
            Mary

Dear Mom and Dad,

My counselor's name is Wally. None of the kids like him. We have nothing in common with him. We don't even know what to talk about with Wally. He is from another generation. Wally is 19.

Your son,

Louis

Dear Father,
    My counselor says never trust anyone over 30.
                Love,
                Terry

P.S. Exactly how old are you?
P.P.S. I still trust Grandma.

Dear Parents,

I feel much better and I have more energy since the counselor started to give us pep pills. I even hit a homerun in baseball.

Maxwell

Dear Mom,

We had a very frank discussion with our counselor in our bunk today about sex.

We told the counselor everything we could.

Norma

Dear Folks,

One of the counselors was caught smoking marijuana. All the kids want to be in his bunk next year.

Your son,
Stephen

Dear Folks,
   They started a campaign for law and order at camp.
   They took away all the water guns.
              Your son,
              Peter

Dear Folks,
   My counselor's name is Ricky. He was in the army and he just came back from Vietnam.
   Ricky says this place is worse.
              Your son,
              Andrew

Dear Folks,
   The counselor hasn't been around the bunk for the last few days.
   I asked the head counselor where he was and he said he was on some sort of trip.

          Love,
             Leonard

Dear Father,
    There's plenty of discrimination at camp and it's all against kids.

                        Your son,
                        Lowell

Dear Mother and Father,
   This camp is too square.
   Nobody has even freaked
out since we got here.
          Love,
            Cynthia

Dear Mom and Dad,
   Ralph Nader should visit
this camp.
   He would close it down
in two minutes.
          Your son,
            Bobby

Dear Mother,

This camp is very different from any other camp I have ever been to.

They do lots of fun things here — especially for us the senior group girls.

Your loving daughter,
Mary

P.S. Please bring my birth control pills up on visiting day.

P.P.S. Better idea would be to send them up special delivery.

Hi!

All the kids in my bunk hate their parents but I am still holding out.

Love,
Philip

Dear Father,
    There are too many rules and regulations at camp.
    Next summer I want to spend my time in a free society.
                    Mark

Dear Mom and Dad,
    Please mail me a book on the Black Panthers.
    It's not on my summer reading list.
                    Love,
                    Cara

Dear Folks,

I am having a great time at camp. Today we had a sit-in at the nature hut and tomorrow we are having another sit-in at the mess hall until they promise to give us chocolate cake at least once a day.

Your daughter,
Linda

Dearest Parents,

My counselor is a lazy, sloppy, rebellious nut. He is my idol.

Love,
Christopher

Dear Folks,
   I hope you will understand but I won't be able to make you a wallet or a belt in arts and crafts this summer.
   All the kids are making peace banners instead.
                    Love and kisses,
                         Diane

Dear Dad,
   This is a very exciting camp. Our favorite activity is praying for a rainy day.
              Your daughter,
                    Annie

Dear Dad,
   Mom asked me to write to
all the relatives.
   Please send me your
Xerox machine.
               Love,
                  Jeff

Dear Folks,
   Last night when the counselor
was sleeping, we tied him up
and shaved off his beard and
gave him a haircut.
   He got pretty mad because
he said now he couldn't go
back to college.   Your son,
                  Sidney

Dear Folks,
    I met a girl at camp that I want to marry when I grow up.
    She's terrific and she doesn't believe in marriage.

                    Your son,
                    Dennis

Dear Folks,

Six of the kids in my group are against the war in Vietnam, five are against Nixon-Agnew and ten are against brushing their teeth in the morning.

Love,
Susan

Dear Dad,
    Last summer our camp play was "Alice in Wonderland".
    This summer we're doing the "Trial of The Chicago Seven".
                    Your son,
                    Harry

Dear Folks,
    We had an election for President of the Campers Club. I won because I made the best campaign speeches. I promised everything.
                    Love,
                    Jimmy

Dear Mom and Dad,
    We had a bikini bathing
beauty contest at camp and
I won the prize as Miss
Camp Pinehill.
    A lot of the girls said I
won because I was the
only one who didn't wear
her top but I think they
are all jealous.
            Love,
            Harriet

Dear Folks,
　　We say our prayers every night before we go to sleep.
　　The counselor has the campers thank God for sending us to this camp. Some of the kids have become atheists.
　　　　　　　Love,
　　　　　　　　Barnaby

Dear Folks,
　　We started a homesick club. So far, we have 30 members and we haven't even had our first meeting yet.
　　　　　　　Love,
　　　　　　　　Karen

Dear Mom and Dad,
  I wrote to President Nixon, Vice President Agnew, Governor Rockefeller and Mayor Lindsay.
  I don't have time to write to the relatives.

           Your son,
           Neal

Dear Folks,
　I'm not homesick for the city anymore.
　One of the kids piled garbage in front of the bunk.

Love,
Donald

Dear Dad,

   I am the editor of the camp newspaper.

   They already banned two issues.

           Your son,
            Joseph

Dear Mother and Father,

   We had our first camp dance last night.

   I didn't dance with any of the boys because I didn't feel any vibrations.

           Love,
            Miriam

Dear Folks,

I'm very lucky this summer. Remember how mad the Counselor used to get at us last summer. When he got mad all the kids had to run.

This year we have a new Counselor and he believes in non-violence.

Your happy son,
Victor

Dear Folks,
   The barber made his annual visit to camp yesterday.
   He left in a hurry after ten minutes.
                Love,
                Roger

Dear Folks,
   To tell you the truth I'm very schizophrenic about camp.
   Some days I hate it and other days I just can't stand it.
                        Love,
                          Cynthia

Dear Dad,
   So far in baseball I have been up at bat 20 times and I have struck out 19 times.
   I have decided to become a coach.
                     Regards from
                        Freddy

To my Parents:
    I, your only son, Victor, Jr.,
being of sound mind and body,
do hereby will my dirty
laundry to you, my parents.
            Love,
                Victor, Jr.

Dear Mom and Dad,
    I won the award for the
neatest kid in the bunk.
I was the only one who
made his bed all summer.
            Your son,
            Lee

Dear Mom and Dad,

The camp owner told us that we should thank our parents for sending us to this camp because this is one of the finest camps in the whole country.

We buried a dead rat today.

Love,
Skipper

Dear Father,
I don't understand why
I am here. Where did I
go wrong?
        Donald.

Dear Father,
I have 102° fever but don't
worry. They have a very good
doctor here. He is not just a
plain doctor. He is a specialist.
His name is Dr. Plummer and
he is a veterinarian.
        Kisses from Mary Ann

Dear Folks,
  This is the last letter I'm
going to write to you.
  I am only interested in
verbal communication.
        Your son and friend,
        Ralph

Dear Folks,
 -This camp has the best
Counselors in the world.
Three of them are conscientious
objectors and five are peace
marchers.
        Your son,
        Roger

Dearest Folks,

   They take very good care of the children at camp. There are two camp psychiatrists.

         Love,
         Nancy

Dear Mom and Dad,
    I'm not eating so good
at camp because they
don't let you watch TV
during dinner.
                Your son,
                    Lawrence

Dear Folks,
    This camp is terrible.
There hasn't been one
demonstration since we
got here. All we do is play
baseball.   Love,
                    Roger

Dear Mom,

Thank you for the homemade apple pie, the cookies and the candy bars. They were wonderful.

Could you please send me some more apple pie? I can get 50¢ a slice.

Yours,

Freddy

Dear Mom and Dad,
  I am a real camp hero.
I went the whole summer
without changing my socks.
  Love,
    Freddy

Dear Father,
    What kind of camp did you send me to?
    They haven't let us sleep until noon yet.
                    Love,
                    Eric

Dear Mom and Dad,
    I don't cry at camp anymore because only sissys cry.
                    Love,
                    Allen
P.S. But I still throw up
        a lot.

Dear Folks,

Our counselor never lets us talk after lights out.

We are beginning to feel like part of the silent majority.

Love,
Susan

Dear Mother,

Yesterday the boys' and girls' camp had nude swimming together.

But don't worry. I remembered what you told me. I didn't go nude swimming. I just sat and watched.

Your daughter,
Patricia

Dear Mom and Dad,
    The camp bugler wakes
us up every morning but
he is really terrible.
    He hasn't played one
rock and roll tune yet.
                Your son,
                Jay

Dear Mother and Father,
    What kind of place is
this camp?
    My tent isn't even air-
conditioned.

            Mark

Dear Parents,

On the very first day of camp all the kids in the bunk agreed that it was wrong to kill any living thing and we took a pledge not to do it this summer.

We have lived up to our pledge except sometimes I wish mosquitoes weren't a living thing.

Love and kisses,
Bobby

Dear Mom and Dad,

Please send me the Wall Street Journal.

I'm getting worried about my investments.

Howard

Dear Mom,
   My bunkmate is a vegetarian. That's the only thing he eats besides his fingernails.
            Your son,
            Adam

Dear Mother,
   This is definitely my kind of camp. It's very sexually oriented.

            Love,
            Sandra

Dear Folks,
  Here is a copy of the official camp newspaper.
  Next week I'll send you a copy of our underground paper.
                    Ronald

Dear Dad,
  We had an election at camp and I was elected camp President.
  I won because I had the best campaign. My platform was to close this camp.
                    Your son, Oliver

Dear Mother and Father,
   I am practicing creative writing at camp. It's called graffiti.

                    Love,
                    Leonard

Dear Dad,
 I like camp. I perspire
a lot.
          Tommy

Dear Mom and Dad,
 Don't worry. They do give
you enough to eat at this
camp if you happen to be
on a weight watcher's diet.
          Your daughter,
          Jennifer

Dear Father,

I am switching my bunk again. This is the third time I have switched my bunk since I got here. And I'm going to keep switching my bunk until I find a bunk where the counselor believes in freedom of speech.

Your daughter,
Barbara

Dear Mother and Father,

Please write me all the news from home but don't bother to tell me about the power shortage, the air pollution, the war in Vietnam or the garbage.

I'm trying to have a good time.

Love,
Susan

Dear Mother,
  Please send me a training
bra.
                    Love,
                      Cathy
P.S. Could you please send
      one that is padded?

Dear Parents,
 The Dramatics counselor
let us pick any show we
wanted for the camp play
with the girls' camp.
 We all voted for "Oh,
Calcutta"!   Love,
        Johnny

Dear Mom and Dad,
 My counselor is pregnant.
Nothing else is new.
        Love,
        Laurey

Dear Folks,

Yesterday was the most exciting day at camp.

One of the kids found a piece of chicken in the chicken pot pie.

Kisses from
Betsy

Dear Mom and Dad,
   I miss you very much but please don't mention it to anybody because it's not "in" to miss your parents.
                Love and kisses,
                Simi

Dear Mother,
   They only give you ham-
burgers, hot dogs and
steak to eat.
   It's a real gyp. We
haven't had beef stro-
ganoff once. Love,
            Sandy

Dear Mom and Dad,
   How are things in good
old New York City?
   Everything is great here
except I'm coughing a lot
from all the fresh air.
            Love,
            Jane

Dear Mom and Dad,
   I received your letter so
I am sending you a picture
of my counselor. Here it is.
The picture is of my counselor
sleeping. You have to be a
very alert photographer
to take a picture of him
doing anything else.
            Your son,
            Arnold

Dear Father,
  The camp counselor is a very mature adult and he reads comic books all day.

          Your son,
            Gerald

Dear Folks,
  I'm not so skinny anymore. Aren't you glad? I weigh 129 pounds.

          Love,
            Tommy
P.S. My friend Freddy got on the scale with me.

Dear Dad,
   What kind of place is this? They want you to play baseball, swim, go hiking and fishing.
   I just came here to do my own thing.
                    Your son,
                    Charles

Dear Mother,
  Camp is a decadent, obsolete, irrelevant, middle-class establishment and I will never return here again.

                    Your daughter,
                        Barbara

P.S. I hope you don't take it too personally.

Dear Parents,
    Yesterday we cleaned up the bunk. We sent the dirty kids to the showers.
                    Richard

Dear Mother,
    I like camp. So far, I already have three soul brothers.
                    Herbie

Dear Mom and Dad,
   We had a talent contest at camp. There were six-teen guitar players and one magician.
         Your son,
         David

Dear Dad,
   Our new counselor, Leon, really loves nature.
   All he ever talks about is going outside to get some grass.
         Your son,
         Roger

Dear Mom,
  I have very nice bunkmates.
One is obviously schizophrenic,
another is a manic-depressive.
There is also a hypochon-
driac and two kids with
claustrophobia.
                David

Dear Mom and Dad,
    A kid in my bunk took this picture of me. He is my very best friend in the bunk. He is a real pal.
                   Tommy

P.S. He wants $5 for the
        picture.

Dear Father,
Last night we had a rock
music festival at camp.
The music was great and
the cops only came twice.
Your son,
Harry

Dear Mom and Dad,
   I like camp very much
but frankly I don't want
to get emotionally in-
volved.
                  Love,
                   Anne

Dear Mom,
   The temperature at camp
was 82 degrees. The air
pollution index was 14.
               Your son,
                 Billy

Dear Mother,
   Maybe I'll learn how to cook at camp because I heard one of the girls say we were going to have a pot party.
                Your daughter,
                Tina

Hi Folks;
This camp is really out of sight.
Even the square kids like it.

Victor

Dear Folks,
Camp is a waste of time. I want to come home and participate in a peace march.

Love,
Tommy

Dear Parents,
   This is the last letter
I will write for a while.
I'm going into a period of
meditation for two weeks.
      Love and Kisses,
         Duane

MAD Humor from SIGNET

- ☐ **MAD'S DAVE BERG LOOKS AT PEOPLE** (#T4951—75¢)
- ☐ **MAD'S DAVE BERG LOOKS AT THINGS** (#T5070—75¢)
- ☐ **MAD'S DAVE BERG LOOKS AT THE U.S.A.**
(#T5043—75¢)
- ☐ **MAD'S DAVE BERG LOOKS AT MODERN THINKING**
(#T4985—75¢)
- ☐ **MAD'S DAVE BERG LOOKS AT OUR SICK WORLD**
(#T4816—75¢)

by Dick De Bartolo, Jack Davis and Mort Drucker
- ☐ **A MAD LOOK AT OLD MOVIES** (#T5036—75¢)
by William Gaines
- ☐ **MAD ABOUT MAD by Sergio Aragones** (#T4619—75¢)
- ☐ **THE BEDSIDE MAD** (#P3520—60¢)
- ☐ **BOILING MAD** (#T4843—75¢)
- ☐ **BURNING MAD** (#T4982—75¢)
- ☐ **FIGHTING MAD** (#T4757—75¢)
- ☐ **GOOD 'N' MAD** (#T5071—75¢)
- ☐ **HOPPING MAD** (#T4844—75¢)
- ☐ **HOWLING MAD** (#T4986—75¢)
- ☐ **IT'S A WORLD, WORLD, WORLD, WORLD MAD**
(#P3720—60¢)
- ☐ **MAD POWER** (#T4952—75¢)
- ☐ **THE MAD BOOK OF MAGIC** (#T5145—75¢)
- ☐ **THE MAD FRONTIER** (#T4981—75¢)
- ☐ **THE MAD SAMPLER** (#P3495—60¢)
- ☐ **MAD'S SNAPPY ANSWERS TO STUPID QUESTIONS**
(#T4987—75¢)
- ☐ **THE ORGANIZATION MAD** (#T4812—75¢)
- ☐ **THE PORTABLE MAD** (#T5118—75¢)
- ☐ **THE QUESTIONABLE MAD** (#T5253—75¢)
- ☐ **THE SELF-MADE MAD** (#P3716—60¢)
- ☐ **SING ALONG WITH MAD** (#T5035—75¢)
- ☐ **THE VOODOO MAD** (#T5042—75¢)